KING COBRA

The Best Advice For Keeping And Caring For A Healthy King Cobra.

Jackson Jose

Table of Contents

CHAPTER ONE 3

   KING COBRA..3

   NATURAL SURROUNDINGS AND LIFESPAN....6

CHAPTER TWO 8

   THINGS YOU NEED TO KNOW ABOUT KING COBRA...8

CHAPTER THREE 32

   KING COBRA INFORMATIONS 32

   THE MOST EFFECTIVE METHOD TO TREAT AND STOP POSSIBLE HEALTH ISSUES 39

CHAPTER FOUR 43

   AVAILABILITY..43

   FUN FACTS 45

   STEP BY STEP INSTRUCTIONS TO CARE FOR A KING COBRA...49

THE END 53

CHAPTER ONE

KING COBRA

The normal size of a king cobra is 10-12 feet. Nonetheless, albeit incidentally, it can arrive at 18.5 feet (5.7 meters). Alluded to as the most significant of all venomous land winds, a King Cobra's width at the neck is of up to 1 foot (0.3 meters). Being thin for the most part, a King Cobra's weight would ordinarily arrive at no more than 44 pounds (20 kilograms).

At the point when completely mature, a cobra is to be hued in earthy colored, dark, green, or yellow. Regardless of their textured skin having a distinct flicker, it's quite dry to the touch.

Normally, King Cobras have whitish or yellowish chevrons or crossbars on their bodies, and their throats differ in shading, beginning from light yellow to velvety, beige-hued subtleties. The King Cobra's midsection could likewise be ornamented with bars; orit will be uniform in an extremely single tone.

Adolescent King Cobras are more modest in size than grown-ups, and that they are glossy, coal black, with their bodies and tails having white or yellow-cross bars.

Likewise, there are four comparative cross-bars situated on their heads.

The significant component recognizing the hamadryad from different cobras is that the accessibility of 11 huge scopes situated on the actual crown of the zenith. Female King Cobras have a total of 239 – 265 ventral scales, while male King Cobras have 235 to 250 ventral scales.

NATURAL SURROUNDINGS AND LIFESPAN

King cobras are dispersed across topographical area and along these lines the Indian subcontinent, from Northern India, and each one the gratitude to southern People's Republic of China, (Hainan and city included), and all through the Malay Peninsula, to the Philippines and western Indonesia. Albeit less generally discovered there, King Cobras are known to occupy territories of East Asia.

King cobras are frequently found close to streams, in bamboo bushes, besides as in open or thick timberlands. They will even be seen in thick mangrove swamps and in contiguous farming zones.

The normal life expectancy of King Cobras kept in imprisonment is 17.1 years, beginning from 12 to twenty years. With wild King Cobras, the normal life expectancy stays the indistinguishable like trained King Cobras – around 20 years.

CHAPTER TWO

THINGS YOU NEED TO KNOW ABOUT KING COBRA

*Caging:

At the point when kept as pets, King Cobras ought to be best given their own personal nooks. As a dependable guideline, a maximum of 1 sets for each walled in area is that the best approach. Lord Cobras are to be just housed together during endeavors for reproducing.

Enclosure should be at least 5 feet in broadness and 10 feet in length. Psyche that the walled in area's legitimate measurement is to affirm that somebody would have the option to uninhibitedly stand, likewise as a move, during upkeep rehearses.

Huge walled in areas are strongly recommendable for King Cobras, for example, for instance, a 16 x 7 x 7 feet (4.9 x 2.1 x 2.1 meter) nook.

In spite of the fact that King Cobras commonly decline to be spurred into entering a crate, having at least one switch box (or lockable shroud box), is vitally significant.

It will in general be trying to dispose of a grown-up Cobra snake from its nook when important, so picking an appropriately planned confine is urgent.

Psyche that when a cobra is given a greater walled in area, it turns into a particular creature than if put during a little pen, when talking as far as conduct. An outsized enclosure will permit proprietors to appreciate truth eminence and insight of Ophiophagus hannan, in light of the fact that the snake is to in a real sense utilize each inch of the confine, having numerous regions to wander.

Climbing openings are fundamental, as well. Ruler Cobras like to spend a long time inside the trees inside the wild, so climbing openings will undoubtedly please spellbound examples. Vining plants, similar to Pothos appended to the enclosure's dividers and falling downwards across the substrate, might be an astounding decision.

*Behavior:

King cobras are astonishingly smart animals, and their conduct isn't any less great. Their temper is both tentative and daring, and everything in the middle. A cobra kept as a pet is even as simple to deal with in light of the fact that it very well might be troublesome, as well.

In view of Ophiophagus Hannah's insight, guardians can build up a truly solid relationship with this extraordinary kind of snake, and this relationship is to just be augmented and made as agreeable as conceivable by guaranteeing to supply the easiest living climate, and by additional keeping high cleanliness guidelines and taking care of practices carefully and dedicatedly.

Except if it's cornered or incited, a Naja hannah would consistently esteem all the more profoundly to get away, rather than to assault, notwithstanding bearing the fearsome standing commonly of the first hazardous snakes out there in light of its lethally strong toxin.

Nonetheless, for settling female King Cobras, assaulting with none incitement is somewhat conceivable.

At whatever point confronted with a danger, a hamadryad can raise the body's foremost part around one meter off the base. When it does as such, it's completely fit for following the foe during this specific, impossible to miss position over some entirely extensive distances.

*Substrate:

All in all, the substrates are frequently mollified into two significant classes. The first is substrate custom-made for bioactive walled in areas, and furthermore the second is all the other things.

In the event that a manager is to pick a spongy, free, non-compacting style of substrate which will be handily supplanted and is furthermore very ease, at that point he/she should take note of that such style of substrate is satisfactory for all, with one primary exemption: bioactive pens.

Non-treated mulch, greenery, destroyed aspen, correspondingly as a considerable lot of the industrially accessible sheet material items, can turn out great as a suitable substrate for King Cobras.

As a general guideline, the substrate should be sufficiently profound to allow the snake to stow away if it's to decide to tunnel.

Business confine lines and papers can get the job done, as well, be that as it may, since King Cobras will in general habitually produce a goliath measure of fluid waste, these don't appear to be the easiest substrate alternatives out there.

Absorbable sheet material is fit for containing the wreck until cleaned. Moreover, it forestalls the Ophiophagus hannan from getting shrouded in dung while slithering through wet paper. During isolate periods or parasites assaults, absorbable sheet material isn't a choice, however.

In enormous pens, fixing bioactive substrates which will assimilate the greater part of the losses without regular purging administrations is completely conceivable. You'll have the option to make the best utilization of free-running Anole species to normally make certain of any flies that typically will in general variety inside the substrate.

For huge, stroll in-sort of fenced in areas, the bioactive substrate is pretty much as profound as 18 inches (45.7 cm). The principal layer might be made out of rocks the elements of a chicken egg.

Then, a sheet of nursery ground texture (water porous) is used, followed up by a layer of pea rock (around 3 inches deep during this specific model).

Upon the layer of pea rock, a layer of manure free, natural nursery soil that is additionally blended in with fine evaluation perlite and vermiculite to ensure appropriate seepage is to be set and finished off with a hardwood mulch layer.

Since hardwood mulch doesn't assimilate water, and it additionally dries decently fast, it's particularly significant during the "wet season." Although there's no genuine "wet season" in charmed King Cobra's pens, you'll impersonate this by coming down on the confines for 1 hour for every meeting, multiple times every day.

*Temperature, Lighting, and Humidity:

It is begging to be proven wrong (in any case) regardless of whether lights that copy common daylight are the easiest decision for right and effective upkeep. Both "delicate white" and "sunshine" fluorescent cylinders can work for giving the truly necessary admittance to light for King Cobras kept in captivity.

Basking lights should be given to gravid female King Cobras.

Contingent upon the season, the first ideal temperature rates for King Cobras can differ yet significantly be the ordinary scope of 82F – 88F (27.7C – 31.1C).

Splashing the nursery with clean water can help cobra managers to expand dampness, correspondingly on copy occasional changes, water the plants (assuming any), and to animate reproducing. A complex alternative is to utilize programmable downpour frameworks, with floor channels to ensure that overabundance water can without much of a stretch break.

Full mechanization will permit hamadryad guardians to appreciate longer with these grand animals, by investing less energy cleaning the pen.

*Diet:

In the wild, the Ophiophagus hannan snake is perceived to follow an ophiogaphy diet, which might be a specific sort of nutritious or taking care of conduct of specific creatures chasing and eating snakes. In a really nutshell, the eating regimen of an Ophiophagus hannan basically comprises of different snakes.

Commonly, in their regular environment, King Cobras select to nibble on non-venomous snakes. Nonetheless, on specific events, they will likewise eat other venomous snakes, including however not restricted to Indian Cobras and kraits.

At the point when food is scant, little vertebrates, similar to reptiles, additionally can change expected prey for King Cobras.

*Eating Habits:

King Cobras gulp down their prey, beginning with the top first. A hamadryad can't bite its prey however all things being equal, it utilizes its top and base jaws, which are appended with stretchy tendons to each other, permitting the snake to swallow creatures that are a lot more extensive than itself.

In the snake's stomach, food is effectively processed as a result of solid acids. Due to their sluggish metabolic rates, King Cobras can live for quite a long time without taking another feast in the wake of having a fundamentally enormous supper.

King Cobras, comparatively to different snakes, utilize their forked tongue to get smells, examining aroma particles so moving these to their Jacobson's organ, which could be a particular receptor that is situated at the mouth's rooftop.

As soon in light of the fact that the fragrance of potential prey is distinguished, the King Cobra's tongue is to in any case flick, checking the feast's course. Lord Cobras even have astounding vision, utilizing it to recognize moving prey very nearly 100 meters (300 feet) away, because of affectability vibrations, and in any case, in light of King Cobras' exceptional prey-track knowledge.

King Cobras kept in captivity do frequently will in general won't eat, if they need been gathered from nature.

As a rule, cobra pets are to require a few bunnies as well as huge rodents consistently, and any snakes are very invite suppers, as well. A larger than usual cobra male may eat more than 5 pounds of snakes and rodents inside multi week however would then regularly take a rest from huge suppers for an all-encompassing time of your time.

*Sleeping Habits:

King Cobras are diurnal animals, implying that they're dynamic by day, in spite of different cobras that will in general be most customarily dynamic inside the night, while not only nighttime.

*Water:

Much the same as ventilation could be an absolute necessity for hostage cobra snake, so might be a huge tub of new, clean water which is needed for both dampness and washing. Water should be changed every day, without any exemptions, and in this way the water tub should be kept up very much cleaned at all occasions.

In the wild, King Cobras are alluded to as superb swimmers.

*Development and Reproduction:

The reproducing season for cobra winds ordinarily happens in late-spring or in pre-summer. Inside the wild, subsequent to mating is finished, the male hamadryad is to get back to its own home, while the ladylike would lay between 10 – 60 eggs.

Reproducing is to begin when a male and a female Ophiophagus hannan snakes are to turn their bodies together, normally remaining during this situation for quite a long time. Prior to laying eggs, the females anticipate around 55 days.

When they're conceived, the cobra posterity are free, all ready to catch their own rodent estimated prey.

Female King Cobras ordinarily mate with a few males, after they develop female leaves pheromones trails for the point of drawing in develop males.

When mating starts, the male hamadryad is to think carefully to rub the underside of the female with the objective to invigorate her.

Female King Cobras lay one grip of eggs every year, making a home out of leaves for the grasp, and covering the home with more leaves before contact top to hatch.

Some King cobras select to lay their eggs under different normal covers, similar to rocks, or in-ground openings. For practically the entire 45 – 80 days of brooding, females would monitor their eggs, their bodies vibrating to concoct heat.

It is just about before the eggs bring forth that the ladylike cobra is to withdraw the home.

CHAPTER THREE

KING COBRA INFORMATIONS

*King Cobra Hatchlings:

The normal size of a Naja hannah hatchling is around 16 to 18 inches in length.

Eggs have abnormally enormous yolks, as a piece of the yolk transforms into a yolk sac that gives the hatchling with around fourteen day sustenance supply, albeit a hatchling is prepared to require care of itself from the absolute first day of its life.

*Maturity:

The pinnacle of development for King Cobras is set apart at the moment they become somewhere in the range of 4 and 6 years of age.

*How To Breed King Cobra:

For hostage King Cobras, reproducing commonly happens from early January to late April. During the brood care period, females will in general turn out to be strangely forceful, so guardians should move toward them with additional consideration and alert.

King Cobra moms to-be ought to be provided with spot lights, with a greatest temperature of 90F (32.2C) to be kept up, while gravid females seldom actually relax. A stepping stool of branches should be likewise accommodated future moms to have the option to thermo-control over an expansive scope of temperatures as they see fit.

*Handling:

In case you're to deal with a cobra snake with an unnecessary measure of certainty, mind that this will be very risky. It's a necessity to utilize proficient security hardware, similar to snares and utensils. On the other hand, a brush or a mop is utilized.

Before truly giving a Naja hannah pet, guarantee to consistently have a medical aid unit accessible available to you, including significant apparatuses against snake nibbles.

Continuously edge and carefully and gradually when taking care of a cobra snake. Astounding, snappy, or potentially sharp developments can undoubtedly unnerve or frighten the snake, bringing about undesirable, subtle activities, and conceivable grievous mishaps correspondingly.

In the event that the cobra snake is to pull back into a S-shape assault mode, stop any endeavors to deal with it right away. Envision it to calm down and to begin moving gradually before you make another taking care of endeavor. Additionally, recall that on the off chance that you're to move gradually and to remain quiet, at that point the opportunities for the cobra snake to remain quiet are much better, as well.

Continuously wash your hands altogether with water and cleanser prior to taking care of the snake, as you are doing not have any desire to debase or to imperil your Naja hannah pet with microscopic organisms and earth.

Wear gloves and defensive gear any time you're taking care of an Ophiophagus hannan snake, as independent of how delicately you're to treat this entrancing animal, there's consistently a chance, regardless of whether somewhat one, for something to travel wrong.

Very sort of like people, Ophiophagus hannan snakes need it moderate alone, and that is extremely evident during their taking care of schedules. Try not to constrain your snake whenever. Be extra cautious when hamadryad is shedding skin, since it will in general be more bad tempered/forceful during this time. Try not to deal with a Naja hannah snake if it's profound sleeping.

THE MOST EFFECTIVE METHOD TO TREAT AND STOP POSSIBLE HEALTH ISSUES

Inside issues, likewise as stoutness, might be forestalled and nullified if hostage King Cobras are to be kept in enormous confines, and gave the genuinely necessary climbing openings. In the event that snakes are kept in too little enclosures, they regularly will in general invest a large portion of their energy inside the shroud box, which further offers approach to stomach related problems in view of absence of activity to emerge.

For recently obtained King Cobras, or for King Cobras moved into a substitution confine, it's basic to lessen any conceivable pressure by allowing the creatures to take as much time as is needed to overview the climate before they get comfortable minus any additional causing them more strain by disturbing them while they're covering up.

Hatchlings are particularly inclined to wellbeing harm if the enclosures aren't to be kept carefully perfect.

Gauging a hamadryad snake is urgent to notice its wellbeing. Simply in the event that you have any doubts about the wellbeing and prosperity of your Ophiophagus hannan pet, promptly contact an expert veterinarian.

With a grown-up, hamadryad snakes, moistening is ideal to be evaded, beside day by day or two preceding shedding however and still, after all that, solitary fog extremely, sparingly. Clouding also as often as possible can cause respiratory diseases.

Hardwood mulch is to prevent the snake from going in consistent contact with the wet substrate, as this may handily bring about skin issues.

Dampness rates ought to be kept up on the high side, with 70% or higher stickiness rates assisting with staying away from eye cap maintenance issues and dry sheds.

CHAPTER FOUR

AVAILABILITY

Most US states, in like manner as different nations across the world, don't let people to keep lord cobras as pets. Be that as it may, in certain nations and in certain states, similar to Florida, it's lawful to keep a Naja hannah as a pet, given you have a yearly license to attempt to do as such.

Buying King Cobras from unlawful retailers/reproducers, or potentially having a cobra without a legitimate license, can end with strong fines, and even detainment.

Keeping a cobra got inside the wild is ill-conceived in many nations, and it's additionally very hazardous to both the snake's, also in light of the fact that the manager's wellbeing and prosperity. Just buy a cobra snake from legitimate retailers, so you and your hypnotizing pet might be conceded a couple of long periods of getting a charge out of a happy, solid, associated relationship together.

FUN FACTS

• The heaviest Ophiophagus hannan example was one gotten inside the wild in Singapore in 1951, gauging 12 kg (26 lb), and estimating at 4.8 m (16 ft). In 1972, a decent heavier hamadryad hostage example, estimating 12.7 kg (28 lb) at 4.4 m (14.4 ft) since quite a while ago, was kept at New York Zoological Park.

• Lord Shiva, the strong divinity, is generally portrayed wearing a cobra neckband.

• Some types of cobras are named after their conduct or appearance, similar to the monocled cobra (N.

kaothia), known to show a positive, monocle-like circle situated on its actual hood, or like the zebra Naja nigricollis (N. nigricincta), having zebra-like stripes.

• Because of the obliteration of woodlands, comparatively as because of the proceeding with illicit worldwide exchange, Naja hannahpopulations have enormously dropped in certain regions of its normal reach.

• In most snake species, females are commonly bigger than the guys. Nonetheless, with King Cobras, male species commonly gauge more, and furthermore are longer, than female species.

• Cannibalism isn't uncommon among King Cobras, and especially in extreme instances of yearning.

• Some specialists are as yet discussing whether King Cobras are diurnal animals. While King Cobras are completely prepared to chase during all times, they're infrequently seen chasing in the dead of night.

• King Cobra males, equivalent to most male cobra species, are to perform exceptional, expound moves when attempting to prevail upon a female cobra's consideration their rivals during the mating season. The one to win these strange rivalries is normally the main male.

- When the eggs are nearly to bring forth, the mother Naja hannah is to rapidly desert her watchman obligations, rapidly leaving the world looking for other prey to try not to eat her hatchlings.

- King cobras are unbelievable slick people, is yet one more strong verification of their astounding insight and instinct.

- Cobra pearls (otherwise known as cobra stones) are bones that are evidently taken from the toxin organs, at that point profoundly cleaned, and acclimated coax toxin out of an injury. In all actuality, the mystical forces of cobra pearls to protract toxin are nothing more except for a legend, and obviously, it's not even certain if the cobra pearls do even come from a snake or on the off chance that they're basically phony.

STEP BY STEP INSTRUCTIONS TO CARE FOR A KING COBRA

1. Develop ruler cobras, and especially hatchlings, do require consistent admittance to scour, freshwater every day. Subsequent

to taking care of, grown-ups frequently drink gigantic amounts of water. On the off chance that a hatchling is to get dried out irreversibly, it can kick the bucket, and accordingly the equivalent can occur if the water source is to contain portions of the substrate in it or potentially if it's not changed as often as possible.

2. Affirm to supply reasonable water compartments that are adequately huge to contain the components of your cobra snake, with respect to the snake to have the option to completely lower.

3. In the wake of being dirty, confines should be cleaned at the earliest opportunity. Doing so will restrict any odds of pollution, on keep the cobra in wonderful wellbeing.

Grown-up Ophiophagus hannan snake produce a lot of fluid with their dung, which infers their walled in area is certainly obligated to defilement. Cleanliness should be kept as high as attainable in any regard times.

4. Without appropriate preparing, King cobras is incredibly perilous to be kept in bondage. It's a prerequisite to regard the reptile's

very own space and to encourage all around familiar with its requirements, requests, qualities, and temper, prior to endeavoring keeping one as a pet.

5. Lighting, temperature, and moistness rates should be appropriately kept up.

THE END

Milton Keynes UK
Ingram Content Group UK Ltd.
UKHW022137080923
428326UK00011B/1086